MOUNT RUSHMORE

Author: Susan Koehler

Rourke

Publishing LLC

Vero Beach, Florida 32964

www.rourkepublishing.com

PHOTO CREDITS: © 77164301: page 5; © National Park Service: page 7, 12, 13, 14, 15, 16, 17. 18, 21; © Library of Congress: page 8, 9, 10, 11, 22; © iofoto: page 8; © pmphoto: page 9, 26; © Michal Koziarski, Eliza Snow: square frames; © Catherine Scott, KMITU: oval frames; © Jonathan Larsen: page 10, 19; © Jody Dingle: page 11; © Amy Nichole Harris: page 19; © John Rivers: page 23; © Wikipedia.com: page 25; © Audrey M.Vasey: page 28;

Editor: Jeanne Sturm

Cover design by: Nicola Stratford, bdpublishing.com
Interior design by: Heather Botto

Library of Congress Cataloging-in-Publication Data

Koehler, Susan, 1963-
  Mount Rushmore / Susan Koehler.
     p. cm. -- (American symbols and landmarks)
  ISBN 978-1-60472-344-1
  1. Mount Rushmore National Memorial (S.D.)--Juvenile literature.
  F657.R8 K63 2009
   978.3/95 22
                              2008014137

Printed in the USA

CG/CG

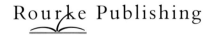

Rourke Publishing

www.rourkepublishing.com – rourke@rourkepublishing.com
Post Office Box 3328, Vero Beach, FL 32964

Table of Contents

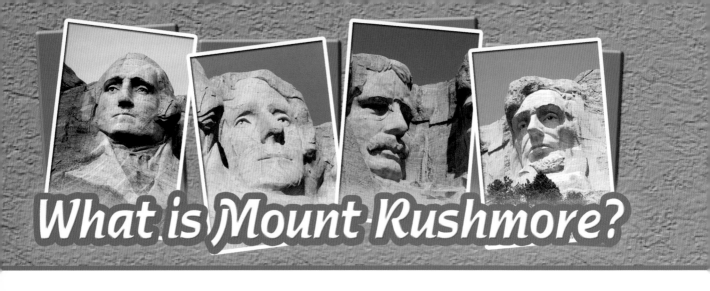

What is Mount Rushmore?

Mount Rushmore is the largest work of art on Earth. It is a sculpture that is carved from granite on the side of a mountain.

Mount Rushmore is an American landmark located in South Dakota. High on a mountain, visitors can see the carved faces of four American presidents: George Washington, Thomas Jefferson, Theodore Roosevelt, and Abraham Lincoln.

The Avenue of Flags at the Mount Rushmore National Memorial displays the flags of all fifty states and six U.S. territories.

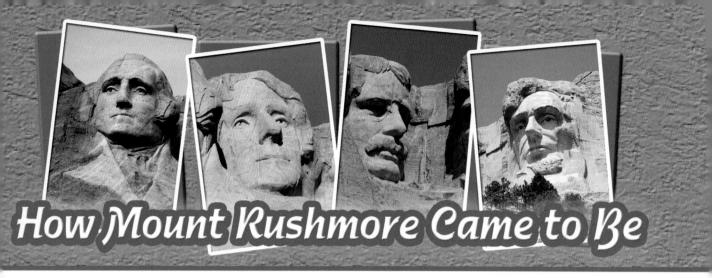

How Mount Rushmore Came to Be

In 1923, a South Dakota **historian** named Doane Robinson wanted to create a monument that would make his state famous. He thought statues could be carved from the rocky **terrain** in a large group of mountains called the Black Hills.

In 1924, Robinson wrote a letter to Gutzon Borglum, a famous American artist. Robinson asked Borglum if he was interested in taking on this **mammoth** project. Borglum accepted the offer. Robinson, Borglum, and others agreed that the sculpture should include the four American presidents we see on Mount Rushmore today.

Gutzon Borglum carefully monitored and inspected all work that was done at the Mount Rushmore site.

7

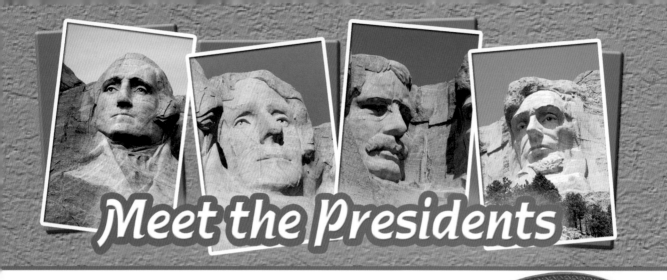

Meet the Presidents

George Washington is remembered as the father of our country. He was born in the colony of Virginia in 1732. After leading troops as a general in the Revolutionary War, Washington was chosen to be the first president of the United States of America.

Borglum chose Washington as a **prominent** figure in the sculpture. Before planning his sculpture, Borglum studied many famous portraits of our first president.

George Washington's head was the first one carved at Mount Rushmore.

8

Thomas Jefferson was born in the colony of Virginia in 1743. From 1801 to 1809, Jefferson served as the third president of the United States. During that time, he purchased land that greatly increased the size of our young country.

Thomas Jefferson was the primary author of the Declaration of Independence and later became our nation's third president.

Borglum included Jefferson in his sculpture because of Jefferson's vision of our country's **expansion**. Because of this vision, Borglum sculpted Jefferson with his eyes pointing toward the sky.

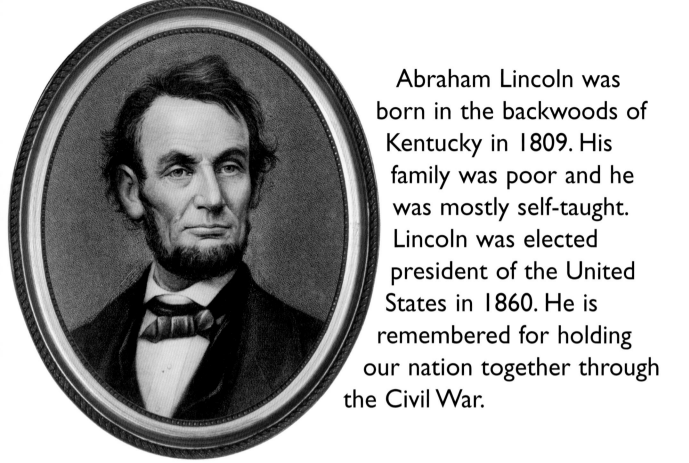

Abraham Lincoln was born in the backwoods of Kentucky in 1809. His family was poor and he was mostly self-taught. Lincoln was elected president of the United States in 1860. He is remembered for holding our nation together through the Civil War.

Abraham Lincoln was assassinated on April 14, 1865, just days after the end of the Civil War.

Borglum admired Lincoln so much that Borglum's only son was named after this beloved president. Borglum studied many photographs of Lincoln, and decided to sculpt him with a **solemn** look on his face.

Theodore, or Teddy, Roosevelt was the twenty-sixth president of the United States. As president, he established the National Park Service. He also made sure the Panama Canal was completed. This canal connects the Atlantic and Pacific Oceans. Borglum admired Roosevelt's boldness and energy.

Before he was elected president, Theodore Roosevelt commanded a cavalry regiment known as the Rough Riders during the Spanish-American War.

Roosevelt and Borglum had been friends, and Borglum sculpted this president from memory rather than photographs.

"Here is the Place!"

Once Borglum selected the figures to be carved, he needed to choose this sculpture's exact location within the Black Hills. Borglum climbed to the **summit** of Harney Peak and discovered the site known as Mount Rushmore. The granite was smooth and the rock faced south, giving it plenty of sunlight each day. After looking closely at the rock, Borglum declared, "Here is the place!"

Calvin Coolidge was the thirtieth president of the United States.

In 1927, President Calvin Coolidge visited South Dakota on his vacation. While he was there, Coolidge made an **ardent** speech, promising that the United States government would help pay for this new American treasure.

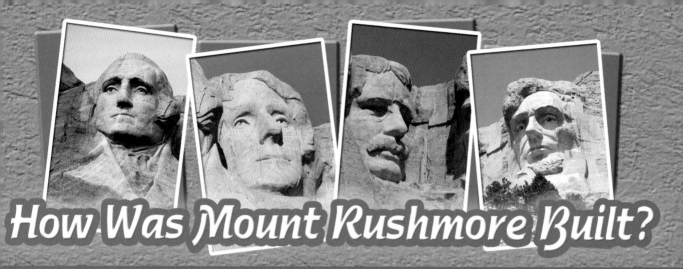

How Was Mount Rushmore Built?

Borglum's work on Mount Rushmore began in 1927. For the next 14 years, over 400 men worked on this project.

14

Workers sat in seats called Bosun's chairs, which were suspended from above.

Most of these men were experienced miners who were looking for work. Borglum's workers built roads, generated power, and removed rock. Large chunks of rock had to be blasted away with dynamite. Workers carved the faces with chisels, hammers, and air-powered drills.

Although the work was dangerous, no one was killed during the **treacherous** task of creating this giant masterpiece.

Workers prepared the carving surface by honeycombing, or drilling many small holes in an area and carefully removing a thin layer of rock.

16

Skilled workers earned $1.25 per hour. This was a good wage for men who were used to working in mines, or who could not find jobs during the Great Depression.

Did You Know?

The Great Depression was a time of economic trouble. This period began in 1929 and lasted until the 1940s. During the Depression, many banks and businesses closed. Millions of Americans lost their jobs, their savings, and their homes. Government projects provided a paycheck for many of these workers.

How Big Are the Faces?

Borglum planned for each head to be 60 feet (18 meters) tall. So, he created a one-inch (2.5-centimeter) to 12-inch (30-centimeter) **scale model** of each president's head. Borglum and his workers simply transferred one inch on the model to one foot on the actual carving.

Each of George Washington's eyes is 11 feet (3.4 meters) wide, and his mouth is 18 feet (5.5 meters) wide.

A comparison can help you understand the size of this work of art. Each president's head at Mount Rushmore is 60 feet (18 meters) tall. Compare this to the Statue of Liberty, a giant work of art whose head is 17 feet (5.2 meters) tall.

17 feet (5.2 meters)

60 feet (18 meters)

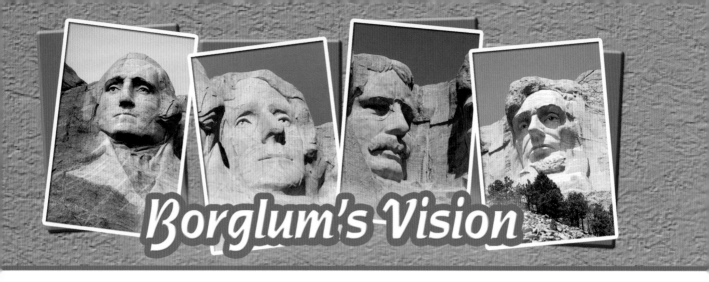

Borglum's Vision

Borglum planned to create statues of each president that included most of their bodies instead of just their heads. He also dreamed of creating a large room filled with historical photos and papers. In 1938, he began carving out a space in the canyon wall behind Mount Rushmore. In this room, he planned to create a Hall of Records.

Sadly, Borglum died in 1941. His son, Lincoln, continued to work on the sculpture. By the end of 1941, the United States entered World War II and all funding for Mount Rushmore came to an end. The Hall of Records was unfinished, and the carvings were left as heads of presidents, rather than the larger statues Borglum had planned.

Borglum's dream of a Hall of Records was completed after his death.

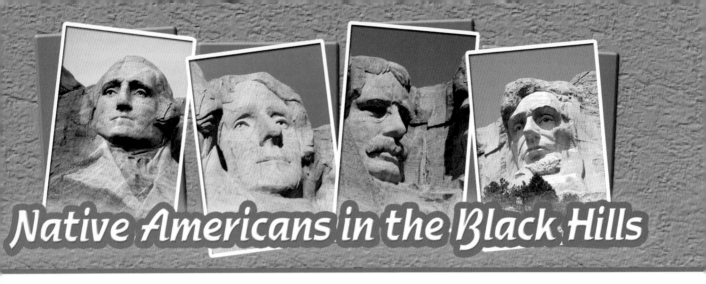

Native Americans in the Black Hills

Sitting Bull was a Lakota Sioux chief.

Thousands of years before the Black Hills held this mammoth work of art, they were home to the **Sioux**. The Black Hills were **sacred** to the Sioux. Famous Sioux leaders like Sitting Bull, Red Cloud, and Crazy Horse had fought and died trying to protect this land.

The Sioux people at one time referred to themselves as the Seven Council Fires.

22

Many Native Americans felt that this land had been unjustly taken from them. They had not always been treated fairly by the American government, so they were not comfortable with this carving of American presidents.

The mission of the Crazy Horse Memorial is to honor the history and culture of Native Americans.

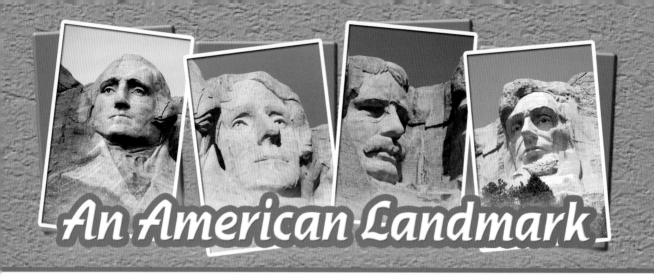

An American Landmark

During the work on Mount Rushmore, several dedications were held. Each time a president's head was completed, there was a ceremony. An official dedication of the entire work of art was planned in 1941. This dedication was never held.

Mount Rushmore Location

South Dakota

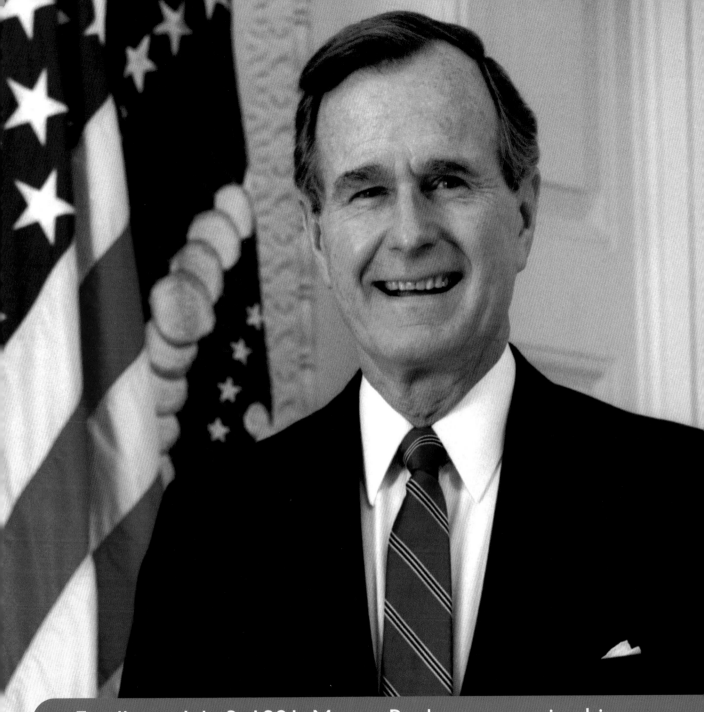

Finally, on July 3, 1991, Mount Rushmore received its official dedication by President George H. W. Bush.

In 1998, the Hall of Records was finally completed. Instead of a carved room, there is a vault behind the statues. This vault contains sixteen panels inscribed with words from historic writings, biographies of the presidents featured on Mount Rushmore, and a biography of Gutzon Borglum.

Each year, thousands of people travel to South Dakota to visit the Mount Rushmore National Memorial. These visitors can enter the Lincoln Borglum Museum to watch a short movie about the monument. They can walk the beautiful Presidential Trail and visit the Sculptor's Studio. And, of course, they can view the breathtaking sculpture.

Mount Rushmore is a remarkable work of art and a
landmark for all Americans to treasure.

Timeline

1885

Charles Rushmore, a New York lawyer, visits the Black Hills to investigate mining claims. Mount Rushmore is named after him.

1924

Doane Robinson writes to American artist Gutzon Borglum about his idea for a giant sculpture in the Black Hills. Borglum agrees to take on the project.

1925

Borglum selects Mount Rushmore as his site and suggests that four American presidents should be the subjects of the sculpture.

1927

President Calvin Coolidge makes a speech pledging government funding for Mount Rushmore. Work begins.

1941

Borglum dies. His son, Lincoln, takes over and finishes the carvings of the heads. The United States enters World War II and has no more funding for Mount Rushmore.

1991

Mount Rushmore is officially dedicated by President George H. W. Bush.

1998

The Hall of Records is completed as a vault containing information about Borglum, Mount Rushmore, and American history.

Fun Facts

Gutzon Borglum was born in Idaho in 1867. His family moved to Nebraska when he was seven years old. When he grew up, Borglum studied art in Paris, France.

Before working on Mount Rushmore, Borglum was carving a likeness of Robert E. Lee on Stone Mountain in Georgia. However, after arguing with the project's sponsors, Borglum left Stone Mountain. His work was cleared and another artist was hired to carve this sculpture.

During his work on Mount Rushmore, Borglum often stood back and viewed the sculpture through binoculars.

Each president's nose on Mount Rushmore is about 20 feet (6.1 meters) tall.

South Dakota's nickname is The Mount Rushmore State.

In 2006, the commemorative state quarter for South Dakota was issued, bearing a picture of Mount Rushmore on the back.

Glossary

ardent (AR-duhnt): filled with strong feeling or emotion

economic (ee-kuh-NOM-ik): having to do with money

expansion (ek-SPAN-shuhn): increasing in size

historian (hi-STOR-ee-uhn): an expert in history

mammoth (MAM-uhth): huge

prominent (PROM-uh-nuhnt): very easily seen

sacred (SAY-krid): holy and deserving great respect

scale model (skale-MOD-uhl): a copy of an object that is larger or smaller than the actual object

Sioux (SOO): a group of Native Americans

solemn (SOL-uhm): very serious

summit (SUHM-it): the highest point

terrain (tuh-RAYN): an area of land

treacherous (TRECH-ur-uhss): dangerous

Further Reading

Bauer, Marion Dane. *Mount Rushmore.* Aladdin, 2007.

Bodden, Valerie. *Mount Rushmore.* Creative Education, 2006.

Patrick, Jean L. S. *Who Carved the Mountain?: The Story of Mount Rushmore.* Mount Rushmore History Association, 2005.

Websites

www.nps.gov/moru

www.pbs.org/wgbh/amex/rushmore/

www.americanparknetwork.com/parkinfo/contentasp?catid&contenttypeid=16

31

Index

About the Author

Susan Koehler is a teacher and a writer who lives in Tallahassee, Florida. As a child, she loved reading mysteries. She liked books so much that she gave up her recess time in elementary school to work in the school library. Beyond the pages of books, she enjoyed listening to stories about the colorful, real-life experiences of her parents and older siblings. Now that she's a parent, she and her husband like to travel with their five children, making sure that every vacation includes at least one grand historical expedition. While at home, Susan Koehler can often be found writing books, playing air hockey, or laughing with her very funny children.